Breaking Into the Light,
A Journey of Self-Discovery and Transformation

Maria Begoña Garcia

Copyright © 2014 by Kwik-Web Publishing House

Written in: 2013 Published in: 2014 Maria Begoña Garcia

All Rights Reserved. No part of this publication may be reproduced, stored in a retrieval system, or transmitted, in any form or in any means – by electronic, mechanical, photocopying, recording or otherwise – without prior written permission by the author.

Kwik-Web Publishing House
Montreal, Quebec, Canada

Cover Design by:
Gordan Blazevic (gordan.blazevic@gmail.com)

Edited by:
David Mercadante (d1mercadante@gmail.com)

Library and Archives Canada Cataloguing in Publication

Garcia, Maria Begoña, 1979-, author
    Breaking into the light : a journey of self-discovery and transformation / Maria Begoña Garcia.

Issued in print and electronic formats.
ISBN 978-0-9936843-2-6 (pbk.).--ISBN 978-0-9936843-3-3 (pdf)

    1. Self-actualization (Psychology). 2. Garcia, Maria Begoña, 1979-. I. Title.

BF637.S4G366 2014	158.1	C2014-906296-6
		C2014-906297-4

Contents

Preface 1

PART I – The Beginning 3

PART II – Chaos 21

PART III – Awakening 61

PART IV – Pearls 79

Preface

January 23, 2005 started out like any other Sunday. I was relaxing at home, and as was our tradition, my brother and his family would be coming over for lunch. That particular week, we also had another guest, Sam, a long-time family friend. Everyone arrived by 2pm and we had a fantastic meal (my mother is an excellent cook). Afterwards, everyone cleared out of my parents' apartment and it was just Sam and me in my apartment downstairs. I was lying on my bed while talking on the phone with my boyfriend – who lived in the U.K. at the time - while Sam watched TV in the living room.

> "Honey, the ocean is near my kitchen table already." What the...?! Did I just say that??? What does that even mean, and why did it come out of my mouth??? "The bed is saying that it's red." HUH??? Now I'm starting to really freak out. And what's with this headache from hell??

I never get headaches... and it suddenly feels like a pressure cooker is ready to blow in my head. "I'll call you later," I manage to somehow say coherently as I hang the phone up. My head is exploding! "Sam!," I call out as I lie curled on my bed. He comes running and must get alarmed when he sees me, because soon afterward my mother is there too.

Out of the blue, a strong feeling of nausea comes over me, and I start to throw up just as my mom gets to me with something to catch the vomit in. "You must have food poisoning," she says. Could be, I had shrimp at lunch and maybe I got sick from it. No one else is ill though, so it could also be something else. I guess I'll find out when the ambulance gets here, I think Sam called them.

PART I

The Beginning

Other than moving to a new continent when I was almost seven, my childhood in Spain was pretty unremarkable. I was born to working class parents where we lived in a tiny village that only had one road with quaint - yet modest - houses along it. I mostly remember those years as happy ones. Besides the time we spent in school, my brother Roman and I - like the other children in the village - were barely ever home. Danger was basically non-existent: we didn´t see much in the way of traffic on the road, besides the occasional cow pulling on a cart. And since the village was small enough so that everyone knew everyone else, there was nothing to worry about in that respect either.

One of my first memories ever is a sad one, though:

> I am three years old and I am standing in abuela's living room. Something really strange happens. Sad people are standing around a

> wood box where abuela is lying down inside! I can tell that her eyes are closed when I see inside of the glass. Everyone is crying and dressed in black (so is abuela), and I know something is really wrong, so I start to cry too. I don't know what is happening, but I know I won't see her anymore. Where is she going now? I'm not sure, but somewhere too far to ever come back, I think. "No, no, no! I don't want to!" I yell at mami because she tells me to kiss the glass that abuela is on the other side of! *Would mom remember any of this today? I wonder...*

Following scene, as mom and Roman are leaving for the funeral:

> I'm standing in the middle of the street, tears falling down my face. "I want to go too!" I say to mami and Roman. "We're just going food shopping," they say to me. It's not true. I know it, I just know it. They're going with abuela. "I want to go too!" I start to panic. *When will **they** come back???*

Fast-forward a year:

When my brother (who is three years older than

me) began going to school, it was held in my neighbor's house, which had a spacious ground floor. All of the village kids - up to third grade - were in the same class. This made it fun and interesting for the youngsters, but I imagine not quite as fun for the teachers. Anyhow, one day I decided to go to school with my brother, and was giddy with excitement on that much awaited morning.

> When I get up this morning, I do everything like mami tells me to. I don't want her to get mad at me and change her mind cause she's letting me go to school with Roman today! It's just on the other side of the street, on the bottom part of my friend's house. He's my secret boyfriend but sshhhhh, don't tell anyone! I'm really excited today because mami says to me I can go too. We go to the other side of the street and see most of the other kids are here, even the big ones that are seven and eight years old. Fun!
>
> The teacher tells me where to sit and I feel pretty special because I get to be with all the big kids in school. And I don't even start for two whole years...that's a really long time! "What's your name?" the teacher asks, and I'm suddenly a star

> because everybody is paying attention to me. "María Begoña García Dieste!" *Oh, oh! Did I say something wrong? I think I have a stupid name because everyone is smiling or laughing... I am getting hot in my face and I start getting sorry that I came.* "And how are you María Begoña García Dieste?" *Duh! Can't you see me?!* "I'M SITTING!" *Oh no, now I really said something wrong! Why is everyone laughing? This is the worst day of my life! I'm never talking in front of anyone again!*

The big joke was that I rattled off my entire given name, of course. But as an innocent child, that could not have dawned on me. And that's how our personalities get fashioned; through an accumulation of stories that seem small and insignificant but ultimately shape our lives. Growing up, I always felt somewhat inadequate and a need to be right before speaking up about anything… that's how I ended up being teacher's pet through most of grade school. It gave me great satisfaction to answer questions correctly, and often. It was my way of getting what I felt was the much needed approval of others.

Anyhow, we didn't see much of my father. He was in the merchant marine, so his job kept him away for months at a time. I don't remember missing him much because we were essentially being raised by the whole village (or by what one could call the tribe). But it was still a joyous occasion whenever he would finally come home after having traveled around for months. He showered my brother and me with the latest gadgets. I still recall the time we got a set of walkie-talkies - what a novelty! We were the coolest kids in town.

This went on for a while, my father being away for long stretches of time. Eventually though, my parents decided the situation was no longer sustainable. My dad had cousins living in the US, and they decided to give it a shot as well, at least for a time so that they could decide if we'd all eventually migrate. I don't know exactly how much longer he lived here than the rest of the family did, but I can remember at least three occasions when my mother left us with relatives in Spain (in separate houses because she knew better...) and went to visit him for a couple of months. The early separation from my parents, albeit temporary, was when I started to grow into a more free-spirited and independent person.

When I was just shy of seven, my parents decided that we'd all move to the U.S. Well, I didn't like the idea one bit, but unfortunately (or fortunately!) I didn't have much of a say at the time. But the unexpected turn my life would later take makes me count my blessings that I ended up moving here.

My father was able to move the rest of the family to

the U.S. – the only thing we had to do to begin the process was visit the U.S. embassy in Madrid and get interviewed. That was easy enough - except that we traveled by train for about ten hours each way. But since we went there and back at night, we were able to sleep most of the time in what I thought were pretty comfortable beds. Then again I was probably way less than four feet tall at the time, so I'm probably not the best judge of that!

We had a cousin living in Madrid, who played tour guide for us for a couple of days. What I remember most of that the trip was spending the day at the zoo. Besides the entertaining stuff though, we got all the paperwork ready for our entry into the US. Things were slowly starting to become more real.

As the departure date neared, the feeling of emptiness inside me grew. Otherwise, I have only vague recollections of the months before embarking on this journey. The one vivid memory I do have is of the big day. It was a late December morning and it was still dusk out. Our belongings were neatly packed and we were ready to catch an early flight to JFK airport with a layover in Madrid. A cab pulled up, and as I got into the back seat, I could only stare out the rear window, in tears and completely heartbroken. What made it even worse was that I spotted my neighbor from across the street, my first childhood love, staring after us out of his bedroom window as we sped away. Wow, I didn't realize the profound effect that had on me – I'm sobbing as I relive the event in my mind. That was the beginning of the wall I've erected around my heart, which I work towards tearing down daily.

During the first leg of the trip, we ended up having to spend the night in Madrid because of a delay that caused us to miss our connecting flight. The same thing happened to a woman my mother knew, whose husband was also living in the States, so we all ended up in a hotel room together for the night. "But I don't want to sleep on the cot!" said Roman. I was the baby of the house though, and naturally somewhat spoiled, so the cot was all his for the night.

The rest of the trip must have been pretty uneventful. Either that or I was in too much shock to remember anything. My next memory is of reuniting with my father at the airport. Although we were all very happy, I still felt like it was an ambivalent moment—I had contrary feelings about the whole thing. I was still too young to fully understand why, but I was unable to shake the grief I felt at leaving everything I had ever known behind.

It took my brother and me about a year to get used to life here, but once we did, it was pretty smooth sailing from then on. Or at least that's what it seemed like at the time. My parents weren't able to adapt to life here though. My father, once he retired from a blue collar job, eventually returned to Spain, and while my mother still lives here, she doesn't speak the language – we lived in a Portuguese ghetto, so she never had to learn English. Her Portuguese is excellent though. Despite not having acclimated to the culture, my parents still worked very hard to provide a better life for us, and to instill us with good values.

I was 13 when I got my first job. It was a summer position at a retail store in the neighborhood. I used the money I saved up on a summer-long trip to Spain the following year, and it was awesome! Then my parents had the bright idea to let me pay my own way whenever I wanted to go back to Spain, which turned out to be basically every summer. At the time, I thought it was a bit cruel on their part. In hindsight though, I understand the lesson they were trying to teach me, and I am grateful for it. I learned how to be self-sufficient, and to go after what I wanted.

I found high school pretty uninteresting. I went to a Catholic school in another town. Since I had various part-time jobs throughout those years, I didn't play sports. In four years, I never felt like I quite fit in. The cool kids were the jocks, and I was just a nerd who had a job. That's not even entirely accurate, since I didn't really fit in with the nerds either. In all honesty, I don't have many memories from that period, at least none worth mentioning. I think I just buried my high school years in my subconscious somewhere. The predominant feeling I have when I think of those years is a sense not belonging.

The Beginning 11

Oddly enough, I was speaking to a friend about high school not long ago, who said that when he went to his reunion he came to the conclusion that everyone felt odd and inadequate during those years. He thought the cool kids didn't speak to him because he wasn't cool, but the cool kids told him they thought *he* was too cool for them and that's why they were afraid to approach him. It's pretty ironic, and just goes to show that at the end of the day, it's all just a matter of perspective.

Around the same time I heard this story, I found an interesting statistic – when asked who should take care of building a child's self-esteem, whether parents or teachers, over 70% of parents said it was the teachers' job and an even higher percentage of teachers said it was the parent's responsibility. Since apparently no one thought it was *their* job, I'd say people would do well to work on themselves, at least those old enough to do so. As for children, I believe it's everyone's job, starting with the parents when that's possible. Just imagine a world where most people are confident enough to move forward with their dreams – it would be a much happier place!

At 18, and after shedding many tears, I was allowed to go away to college. I ended up going to a school in New York State, which allowed me to come home whenever I needed to do some laundry and raid the refrigerator! All kidding aside, it was basically a compromise I reached with my parents in which I could dorm at school but still be close enough to home for their taste. Going away to college meant having to take student loans. With the strong work ethic and sense of responsibility I had developed in my teens, I was able to pay these off the summer I graduated.

I loved my time in college and think of those as some of the best years of my life. I was on the crew team as a freshman, and although I enjoyed the sport, I dropped it at the end of the year. Practice was at 5:00am every weekday morning, and frankly, that put a bit of a hamper on my social life. I wanted to enjoy the party aspect of college too, and doing both wasn't really working out very well for me. On that note, I remember getting up one Saturday morning for a crew meet and going out in the hallway to get the clothes I had left in the dryer overnight. *That's hysterical,* I thought as I rubbed my eyes from sleep; someone had hung women's underwear from every water sprinkler. But the joke was on me, as I came closer only to realize they were mine!

I was swim team manager the next three years - mostly because I wanted to take advantage of the early registration that athletes were privy to. I'm an actual swimmer now, though I only took it up about 4 or 5 years ago.

I studied abroad for my first semester junior year. Lo and behold, I went to Spain. Not very original on my part, but I had always yearned to live there again. This time, I was in Madrid, which is similar to NYC though much smaller – a mini version of the "city that never sleeps." And I mean that in the most literal sense of the word... I refer to my time spent there as "party abroad." To give you an idea, the city subway system shuts down daily between the hours of 2 and 6am, which was never of any consequence to me since I was never home before 6am on nights I went out, which was pretty frequently. Anyway, while in Madrid, I took advantage of the proximity and ended up in my hometown – it was less than an hour away by plane. Since I had been going there practically every summer since coming to live in the U.S., it was more of a return home than anything else.

I came back to the U.S. for my last semester at college. After four years and many fun adventures, I graduated at the top of my class. This was a huge achievement for me since I was the first in my family to graduate college. I thought about immediately getting a job in my field, but then decided a wiser move would be to go live in Europe for a little while. After all, I had my whole life ahead of me to work.

So I decided to go live in Germany, and learn the language simultaneously. My reasoning went something like this: I majored in Finance and in International Business, and since I didn't want to enter the world of work just yet, I could learn a language and live in Europe at the same time. German seemed like the rational choice because the Euro is based on the

German mark, so learning the language would eventually be beneficial to my future career in business. Besides, I thought, since Germany is in Europe, it's probably similar to Spain. As I found out the hard way, that couldn't be further from the truth regarding the social aspects of the society. Nevertheless, I had a fantastic experience the two years I spent in Munich.

After college graduation, and a few months before the start of my trip, I was waitressing at a diner in Manhattan. As summer was nearing its end, my boss' friend came in for a visit with another friend of hers who, as it turns out, was from Munich and was now spending some time in New York. He ended up giving me contact info for some of his friends at home, which I was extremely grateful for since I didn't know a single person there. Things were off to a good start!

Since I had worked all summer, I had enough money to live off of for about three months. So my master plan was to find some way to support myself beyond that once in Munich. To get there, I wound up buying a round trip ticket without the intention of using it, but rather because it was cheaper than a one way flight! My self-imposed three month "trial" period was longer than the time frame of the round trip anyhow.

I was happy and looking forward to the wonderful world of possibilities when the departure date in November came. My nervous family - who thought I was insane for moving to a different country where I didn't know a single other person - came to see me off at Newark airport. They didn't understand why in the world I was just picking up and leaving, but the decision was perfectly typical of the independent, self-determined and somewhat stubborn person I was, so they weren't shocked. Once aboard a Lufthansa aircraft headed to Munich, it dawned on me that I had better decide where I was staying when I got there - that's how much of a plan I had! This prompted me to flip to the hotel pages in my Lonely Planet Munich travel guide and just pick a place, one that seemed pretty central and easy to get to from the airport. I did have an interesting time getting to the hotel, but mostly because of my two suitcases.

The atmosphere at the hotel was a bit somber, yet I decided take a chance anyway. After I got settled in, I proceeded to find a pay phone and call Lotte, the only person I *knew of* in Munich, being a friend of the guy who I had met at the diner. I never did find out from Tom if he had told her to expect my call. In any case, she was fairly nonchalant about my reaching out to her and spoke English fairly well, much to my relief. She invited me out that very night (Friday). I met her at her apartment, which just happened to be pretty close-by, and was totally unplanned on my part. *Coincidence?*

Lotte was living with two other women, who were also in the same college, and we all headed to a university party. Other than feeling a bit out of sorts because of the language and the jet lag (and the fact that I was by far the shortest one there - these Germans were tall!), I had a nice time. They dropped me off at the hotel at the end of the night and told me to check out the next morning and go live with them while I looked for my own place. And that's exactly what I did! Thinking back on that time, I'm still in awe at the way life perfectly unfolds when we allow it to.

All three girls were extremely helpful; they answered an ad they found in the newspaper seeking a female roommate. And within a couple of weeks I was living in a new, centrally located apartment, with a native German who was around my age. I also found a job right away; as the girls had suggested, I applied for work at an Irish restaurant on the main avenue. It didn't matter to the owner that I couldn't speak a lick of German because I ended up getting the job! And that's how I supported myself for the next two years. I learned tons of German through working and interacting with customers. The girls also helped me enroll in a language school where I had class five days a week for three hours a day. I did this pretty much the whole time I lived in Munich.

Suzanne, my new roommate, was good-natured and personable. We hit it off immediately. I also started dating an amazing man who was always willing to lend a hand, - we were together for almost the whole time I was in Germany - and made excellent new friends. The entire trip ran incredibly smoothly…I couldn't have orchestrated it better myself! In hindsight, I attribute the flow I experienced to my total lack of worrisome thoughts regarding my overseas adventure, for worry comes from the verb "to strangle." I did not "strangle" the good that was coming my way by worrying.

When I finally returned to the U.S. after my two year stay in Munich, I suffered a bit of what's known as reverse culture shock. It was great to be back, yet as time went on, I missed being in Germany more and more. Not to mention I was living at home with my parents again and that got stressful pretty quickly. After a month or two I found work as a secretary at a post-production company a friend of mine worked for, which helped me dig myself out of the hole I was falling into. That gig lasted a few months - until I got fired that is. It was my first "being fired" experience, but it didn't take long for me to realize that it was actually a good thing.

I was waitressing again at my next job. To this day, I still consider waitressing to be one of the most fun jobs I've ever had – and this was at probably one of my favorite locations. It was a Mexican bar/restaurant in midtown Manhattan, near the United Nations in New York City. I spent a fantastic four months there, and got to meet some of the most interesting people. I was also making substantially more money than as a secretary while doing something I found far more interesting.

At the same time, the apartment building where my parents had been tenants for over twenty years went on the market. They thought about renting an apartment elsewhere, but because mortgages and rents were in the same price range, I told them that I'd just be living with them until I got back on my feet if they planned to rent again. On the other hand, if we bought a duplex, we could each live on one floor and make alternate mortgage payments.

Soon afterwards, before we even began actively searching, we came across a for sale sign on a cute two apartment home. The owners at the time were moving to Europe and we decided to jump on the opportunity. A turn of events in the near future would make me realize what a fantastic decision that turned out to be.

I then landed a position working in a brokerage house. Now that I think about it that was also something that just fell in my lap. My brother's friend - who was already working there - put in a good word for me, so I was quickly called in for an interview after sending in my resume. When I got to the building the morning of my appointment, I was pretty nervous. I hadn't interviewed in a while, and didn't really have any specific skills to speak of – I'm a really good waitress? Probably wouldn't fly.

I arrived a few minutes early and decided to chit-chat with some of the people there, who told me that I had been assigned to the most difficult interviewer at the company. *Holy &#*@!!! Why on earth did they just tell me that...?! As if I wasn't a bundle of nerves already...* But the next thought that came to mind was, *why even bother worrying? It's going to be what it is, there's no sense in getting even more worked up.* And just like that, I regained some sense of composure. The operative word being some...

Finally I was called in. The interviewer, Alona, looked like she was all business. She was dressed very professionally and had a very matter-of-fact air to her. And then, *score!* To my utter amazement, we ended up having a half hour conversation about my life in Germany. At the end of the "interview," I felt – more than anything - like we were old friends. Needless to say, I was offered the job - an entry level position doing client account maintenance at a brokerage house, which I accepted. And the job site was less than half hour from home door to door! Soon I became a rising star in the company, getting a Series 7 license (stock broker license) within five months, and on the heels of which was a promotion. Things were going great...until life thought otherwise.

PART II

Chaos

The rest of the events of January 23, 2005 are blurred, though I'll be as precise as I possibly can.

Since there had been a pretty big snowstorm a few days earlier, the roads were covered in feet of the white powder. When the ambulance finally arrived, they briefly looked me over. I remember them asking me things, and me responding, yet I know I was saying things other than what I meant to say...how strange to realize that the words coming out of your mouth are not at all the ones you had intended on speaking. It was like I was watching myself as if I was a third party, and noticing the total disconnect between my thoughts and words.

The responders apparently didn't think anything too serious was going on, though, despite my face being visibly affected (that's the overall impression I have of their visit). And since we had had shrimp at lunch, my mother also thought I was just having a violent reaction.

In any case, the ambulance did not take me – something about getting to the hospital faster if someone else drove me there because of all the snow. I also know I spoke to my brother, who had left for work an hour before the commotion began, either before or after the ambulance came. He no longer remembers this, and all I remember was thinking that something was seriously wrong with my speech…

Sam called Jose - another family friend who lived nearby - for a ride to the nearest hospital, which fortunately was less than five minutes away. I had extreme vertigo and was not able to walk to the car without help, so mom and Sam each got on one side of me as we walked over. They packed me into the back seat and we all rode to the emergency room. I don't remember the short car ride there at all. Once in the emergency room, I waited for what seemed like an eternity to be seen; all the while my condition was rapidly deteriorating.

The rest of the day is very foggy; I only remember bits and pieces of it. I know I was questioned and – according to hospital records - still managed to respond somewhat coherently. I also remember getting some type of a head scan.

> "We think you may be having a stroke," someone who I think is an intern says to me. "We have to transfer you immediately to UMDNJ

> hospital." My head is floating and I'm too confused to even ask, so I just nod in acceptance. But *what's a stroke? I've never heard that word before. I wonder what it is.*

And that wasn't me forgetting the meaning of things. I really didn't know what a stroke was; the word just wasn't in my vocabulary at the time…

Since the first hospital was not equipped to deal with stroke cases, I was rushed to another hospital where—besides having a catheter inserted—I spent the night without receiving any treatment. I believe the right people weren't able to get to the hospital on a Sunday evening, especially with so much snow on the ground. The following morning, a procedure was performed, where a device known as a balloon was inserted through my groin and up into my brain to bust the clot - which turned out to be five millimeters long… The #1 doctor across the country for this surgery was assigned to me.

> A chill comes over me as I lie naked on a cold metal sheet. *Aren't these used for autopsies?!* How reassuring… I wish they would just cover me so I can stop shivering and not feel so damn vulnerable. People walk all around me but I am invisible; nobody pays me any mind. I want to

> *go to the bathroom! I scream. Please bring me a bed pan, take me to a bathroom, anything...! I can't hold it in anymore. PLEASE!! But wait, they can't hear me... Why won't my words come out? Can't they see I have to pee? After what seems like eons, I don't have the strength to hold it in anymore and I just release my pelvic muscles. Ah, that feels amazing. And at that very moment, the anesthesia kicks in and I lose consciousness.*

It wasn't until that very moment that I actually noticed my ability to speak had vanished over-night…

Despite the brilliant surgical team, my family outside the operating room was told that there was a strong possibility that I wouldn't survive as the odds were very unfavorable; apparently the mortality rate was 100% for people who didn't have the procedure, as opposed to 70% or 80% for those who did. Funny thing is, the morning of my operation, I felt perfectly fine. My head was clear and I was able to think without any mental fog whatsoever. That same morning, a good friend had come by to tell me my boyfriend would arrive from London within a day or two. And I innocently thought that I'd only be in the hospital for just a few more days and would be able to spend some time with him at home.

The operation to break through the clot was considered a medical success, but that isn't what it felt like from my perspective. I could hear and see everything around me, but on top of not being able to speak, I now couldn't move at all either (a condition known as locked-in syndrome in medical jargon). Everyone thought I was in some type of vegetative state (or coma vigil), and medical professionals did not hesitate to tell my family that I'd stay that way for the rest of my life, as such a state is a chronic or long-term condition. In the vegetative state, patients can open their eyelids occasionally and demonstrate sleep-wake cycles. They also completely lack cognitive function.

> What in the hell is going on with me? I can see and I'm aware of everything happening around me, but everyone acts as if I'm not even here, as if I'm in some kind coma. Hello? I'm here?! Why can't I talk or move?! Unreal, this isn't happening. Am I really trapped in my own body? Not even, because I no longer command it. I'm really trapped in my own head...! My confusion soon gives way to frustration and anger at my total impotence. Lord, please help me! How long is this going to last?

And shortly thereafter, my boyfriend arrived in the U.S. I know that during his brief stay he often came to the hospital to be with me, yet I only vividly remember one of those times:

> *"I'm going to read you a letter I wrote last night as I sat alone in your apartment thinking about us," he says to me, hoping that I hear him (but I can tell he doubts it) as I lie expressionless on the bed.* YES, I'm listening baby! You have no idea how much it means to me that you're here. I know I haven't told you yet... I love you. I really love you. Why is this happening right now?! *"...when you get out of here, I'm taking you back to London with me. And I'll take care of you, you'll recover..."* Please stop crying baby, this is tearing me up inside... it's unbearable to think he has no clue I'm even listening.

We would eventually split up though; the situation became too intense for him to bear. He was only 24 years old and was living 3,000 miles away. And honestly, it was too intense for me as well.

He went back to London after a few days. And my days just all began running into each other, becoming a blur of sameness, like a scene out of the movie Groundhog Day.

> Medical students parade through my room on a daily basis with an instructor who pinches my leg seriously *hard* to show how I don't react. *OOOOOOUUUUUUUUCH!* You @#$?!!!! *Let me pinch you like that. AAAAAAAHH!* Little does he know how much it hurts, if he could only hear the screaming and cursing in my head...

I also vaguely recall organ donation people speaking with my family soon after my boyfriend had left. I can't even begin to imagine what it must have done to them. To this day, we haven't openly talked about any of it; the wounds still run too deep. Furthermore, a number of complications arose a couple of weeks after the surgery. For one, my brain swelled a great deal. Then I had an all-over rash that no one could find the cause of. What had initially been confusion, anger, and frustration was quickly turning into grief at the realization that I was in way more serious trouble than I thought.

Sometime after my surgery (I can't remember how long exactly, it could have been days or weeks), one of my girlfriends – Susana – realized that I was actually conscious of everything that was going on. She was showing me pictures of a trip I took to Brazil to visit her during her semester abroad in college. I recognized the photos and remembered everything, but was unable to communicate that in any way. *If there is a place called hell,* I thought, *this must be it.* It was the look of awareness (mixed with desperation) in my eyes that finally told her I was in there somewhere. Words can't describe my relief the moment the fact that I was conscious dawned on her. It was like being rescued from invisibility, or better yet, like I stopped being some kind of inanimate object.

> Yeeees! Someone finally figured out that I can hear, that I'm aware of what is going on around me. Tell the others, please hurry! This way they can try and figure out how to get me out of this mess...

Susana told my family, and soon after, everyone (including doctors and nurses) knew that I was "there." And that's when the real fun began.

In the interim, I had had plenty of time to think about my grueling predicament. What a torment to be fully cognizant yet realize the impossibility of *any and all* communication at the same time. As things stood, death was looking pretty good. Yet I can't say I was ever truly petrified because deep inside I felt this was somehow transitory. It was more like pure desperation and anguish in the moment. But I never thought that I was destined to live confined to a bed forever. Yes, that's exactly it. It wasn't so much that I thought I would recover; It just never crossed my mind to think that I wouldn't...I simply hadn't thought that far ahead. That preoccupation wouldn't rear its ugly head until later.

My first real communication with the outside world took place when someone thought to tell me to blink once for yes and twice for no. Although it was some sort of break-through, misery didn't even begin to explain my state...

In the days that followed, a miracle occurred. I began to lift my right index finger about half a millimeter, which helped my brother come up with a new way to communicate with me. I'd actually spell things out for him - he'd go through the alphabet, after having asked me if the letter fell between A and M. If I blinked yes, he'd spell the letters one at a time beginning with A. If I blinked a no, he'd start spelling at the letter N. Then he scrutinized my right hand for the barely perceptible upward motion of my finger to confirm that he'd arrived at the right letter. This was pretty time consuming, as you can imagine, and frustrating as heck.

All I could think about was my present state and how tormenting it was. I wanted nothing more than to be dead and was actually cursing the fact that I had managed to survive. *What's the sense in living like this???!*

I'm not sure when precisely, but during another one of her visits, I somehow managed to communicate to Susana – repeatedly – that I wanted her to kill me. She would tell me years later that that had been a really emotional experience for her. Another time, my father was with me for one of his shifts. Nothing different had happened but I was in a particularly black mood. So I proceeded to spell out "I want to die" for him in Spanish three times. Just thinking about it now makes me cry. As if it were not enough to have your only daughter immobilized and mute in her twenties, she throws that at you, twisting the knife in your heart further and further. I'm too ashamed to ask him about this, but I'm pretty sure it's been burned into his memory.

Speaking of "shifts," I'd like to comment on how supportive and nurturing my family was. I wouldn't be where I am today if it weren't for them. The three of them, my parents and my brother, took a shift each a day in order for someone to be with me around the clock during my initial hospitalization, which lasted close to two months. It means the world to have people show up like that for you. And my family is not the type to say anything loving or sentimental, but they were there when it counted. Let me tell you, it was quite humbling to have my brother help me with the bed pan. I will never be able to adequately express in words the gratitude I feel for all they've done for me.

Actually, I wouldn't be here at all if it weren't for my family. Since they took turns to be with me around the clock, I was never alone. One night, a couple of days after I was taken off the ventilator (tube inserted in through the mouth that breathes for you) and moved out of the intensive care unit, I began to choke in the middle of the night. My mom raised the alarm and I was immediately rushed away and put back on the respirator. If she hadn't been with me, no one would have noticed in time to save me.

Here's what I remember of the night:

> I'm startled out of sleep from a lack of breath. My body begins to convulse as I start coughing and gasping for air. I know mom is there, and suddenly, there's commotion all around. In an instant, everything goes black. I have a deep sense of peacefulness. *Am I dead?* BLISS. And in what seems like a millisecond and an eternity at the same time, I come to with the realization that I'm lying on a hospital bed with that damn tube in my mouth again. *NO, NO, NOOO!* It's not all a horrible nightmare. This really is my life now, or what's left of it.

Eventually, I got a tracheotomy. Unfortunately for me though, only after having first become all too acquainted with the ventilator (or endotracheal tube); it was inserted into my windpipe through my mouth. For the most part, these are used on short term cases to avoid undergoing a surgical procedure. I'm still not sure why, but I had one for about a month. It was fixed to my face with tape, which was removed daily for cleaning. Not only was I in extreme discomfort because of the foreign object halfway down my esophagus, but it would hurt like hell when the tape was yanked off my cheeks. I'd start to cry in anticipation of the dreaded cleanings every time I saw a nurse walk into my room holding gauze and the other cleaning supplies. I can still feel a hand tugging at my tongue through a gauze pad – which kept it dry and prevented it from slipping from the nurse's grip – as the tube was rammed down my throat amid incessant coughing and gagging day after day; it was absolute torture.

For some reason, I was given Percocet (unbelievably enough, not due to the trauma inflicted on me with the breathing tube every single day). Soon after I realized that they were a great way to escape my reality for a bit; so I developed a bit of a taste for them (to say the least). I started claiming I had severe headaches daily, and was given fistfuls of the light blue pill. Someone must have eventually caught on though because I suddenly started getting extra-strength Tylenols (or something similar) instead. "*Bummer, the gig's over,*" I thought. Actually, I didn't take it as lightly as I'm making it sound. But it's not like I was in a position to really do much about it.

I also recall the day my brother spoke to me about going on Prozac. He went through all the risks and repercussions. And despite the negative connotations/ consequences the drug might have for me, I motioned to him that I wanted to try the antidepressant. I was consumed with dark thoughts and was constantly crying. In the so-called real world, I would have been considered dysfunctional. Antidepressants helped me temporarily deal with the life that was so heavily weighing on me at that moment.

At some point during my extended stay in the hospital, I caught a serious case of MRSA, which is a super-bacterium. My case was especially resistant; so much so, that the hospital had to get special permission from the state to treat me with a certain drug. I was especially amused with the funky yellow gowns my visitors had to wear. **Please put your biohazard suits on people, you are at high risk of contamination.** As if I already didn't feel like some kind of freak…

Around this time, I was sitting upright in bed (with help) and was able to move my right arm and fingers. And to demonstrate this, I was all too willing to give every doctor the middle finger each time he walked into my room. I'm embarrassed by it now (I'm really not actually…) but that's how frustrated I was with everything. Being stuck inside those four walls just exacerbated an already horrible situation. It was also my way of saying "that's what I think of your and your colleagues' prognosis."

So even though what had started only as the ability

to slightly move one of my fingers had turned into the ability to move most of the right side of my body, the left side remained paralyzed. And I still wasn't able to speak at all. My brother then had the ingenious idea of bringing me my laptop. The sense of relief was indescribable. To say that I felt as if a tremendous weight had been lifted off my shoulders is a sore understatement. I was finally able to fully communicate by slowly typing into a Word document with my right hand. I felt liberated, no longer bound by the confines of my uncooperative body.

By this time, Roman was giving me a significant amount of physical therapy on a daily basis, which he had started doing to a limited degree soon after my initial procedure. The therapy consisted of him bending and stretching my limbs in all sorts of directions. He had thoroughly researched strokes (which he verified for me when I interviewed him for this book) and found out that early movement is crucial to recovery.

Since my left foot didn't budge and only pointed straight down, like a ballerina's, it had to be casted in order to reacquire any range of motion. This is known as serial casting – because it consists of a series of casts over a couple of weeks. Each cast progressively held my foot in a more upright position, which was pretty uncomfortable. It reminded me of wearing braces as a teen and the feeling in my mouth whenever I had them tightened, which forced the teeth to shift (except this time it was with the bones on my foot and ankle).

By this point, the whole situation became incredibly surreal to me. Here I was, with a fully functioning brain, yet unable to so much as swallow. I remember that during a friend's visit once, I even typed out that I felt like I was in an episode of the Twilight Zone. I was the same person on the inside, yet totally different on the outside. I was living in a bad dream that I couldn't wake up from. I now began to seriously reflect on my life – I thought about the long and difficult road that lay ahead and sank further and further into my depression. My attending physicians didn't exactly help with my state of mind either.

> Doctors come in and out of my room all day long; I must be pretty freakin' interesting. There is one doctor who's in mental health, perhaps a psychologist or a psychiatrist. She comes to see me often and asks how I feel. What do you think lady??? I've been cooped up between these same walls for over a month. Not to mention that I haven't showered or eaten since I got here. So yeah, I've seen better days... "When you're home, things will be different, you'll be different." What does she mean "*different*"?

I'll never forget those words. It was the first time the

possibility of anything but a full recovery slowly, yet powerfully, crept into my mind. Now I understand why in some places, severely ill patients aren't told the entire truth about their condition. For one, it robs you of any semblance of peace you might have had; and two, it oftentimes becomes a self-fulfilling prophecy.

I'd jump from one extreme to the other; at some moments I'd think that I had been chosen for something bigger than myself, and at others that I had gotten royally screwed (which was really the predominating feeling).

> How did this happen, God? Why me? How did I go from travelling alone all over the globe one moment to being completely helpless the next? What did I do to deserve this?!

That was my "why-me" stage, which went on for much longer than I'd like to admit. I was the victim; a casualty of the cruel world we live in. I wanted people to feel sorry for me, to commiserate with me. That's what I was now hinging whatever feelings of self-worth I still had left in me on. The sympathy of others made me feel like I was still relevant somehow.

For the most part, people who suffer strokes end up paralyzed on one side of their body. I believe that's what the psychiatrist was primarily referring to when she said I'd be different. And so this was the state I lived in for a while, but the ability to move gradually returned. Yes, to this day, the right side of my body is stronger and I limp ever so slightly on the left. If I had to give it a value, I'd say right now I'm about 85-90% recovered though. I really believe that a big part of my extraordinary recovery was that I didn't *know* that I shouldn't have been able to regain my mobility. This illustrates the power of belief, which I'll talk more about in detail later.

> Yes, I can finally get out of this hospital! Granted, it's to go to another facility; but this is different, it's a rehab center. Roman told me it's where Christopher Reeve went when he had his spinal cord injury. He also says that they really want me as a patient there, to the point of competing against other rehab centers. So I know it's going to be great. They'll patch me right up, and after all is said and done, I'll finally be able to look back on all this as just a bad memory. Things turned out a bit different than I imagined they would at the time, though.

After 43 long days, l left the hospital for the first time since my stroke; the place where the days had just blurred into one another out of the sheer monotony of lying down 24 hours a day. My initial feeling was one of quiet contentment and relief at finally not having to stare at the same ceiling day in and day out. I then became excited and curious too; I knew this place was going to be very different from what I was leaving behind.

Upon my arrival, I was checked in, put in the room I'd be sharing with another person, and was seen by the head neurologist. I would be evaluated in the morning so a treatment protocol could be designed.

My evaluation at the new site the next morning impacted me tremendously. I can still see Erica (the therapist) as she put a hairbrush in my right hand, the one that I could move slightly, and told me to brush my hair. The second I noticed I couldn't even bring the brush near my head, I began crying like a baby out of complete desperation, and couldn't stop for the rest of the session. The reality of it all hit me like a ton of bricks. It became instantly clear that the dream I had of walking out of the rehab center as if nothing had happened was an illusion. The psychologist's words rang loudly in my ears, and I spent much of my two months at the center in tears.

On a more positive note, my family (really my mother) no longer stayed with me overnight once I moved into the rehab center. This made things much easier on them and how they alternated shifts. The highlights for me - if you can call them that - were the removal of my breathing and feeding tubes. First they removed the tracheal tube (breathing tube), and once the hole in my throat where it had been sealed itself, the feeding tube was taken out too. And when that happened, I was finally able to really eat again! It was the most incredible thing for me to savor food and feel the wetness of a drink inside my mouth, even if everything had to have the consistency of honey while I relearned how to swallow, including water. Boy did I love those pureed pancakes with syrup though!

The TV in my room was on all day, and it had been an enormous source of grief for me to constantly watch food commercials while yearning for the pleasure of tasting something - of tasting anything! Of course, I couldn't change the channel, nor could I tell anyone to change it for me, at least not at the first hospital. So my new favorite food when I began eating again became ice cream. Later on it became anything I could get my hands on, which eventually led to me gaining about forty pounds – twenty to get back to my normal weight, and an extra twenty on top of that. My brother tells me that he couldn't believe the quantities of food I ingested. I was actually shocked when I looked at myself in the mirror one day only to realize how much weight I had gained. To me, it felt like I looked skinny and sickly one day (sitting upright once, I actually got scared looking down at the toothpicks attached to my hips), and like a blimp the next. Granted, twenty pounds doesn't sound like much, but on a 5'2" frame, it's pretty substantial. Anyhow, it was when I recognized how heavy I'd gotten that I started making a conscious effort to lose weight, and was able to get back to my normal size.

While at the rehabilitation facility, my family decided I would try acupuncture. I wasn't too excited about having needles stuck on my skin, but by this point, it didn't really faze me much. I was also willing to do anything that would improve my health somehow. Acupuncture primarily ended up helping with spasticity (which is unusual tightness or increased muscle tone), - in addition to helping with function and mobility loss. I continued acupuncture treatments for years after leaving the center and became friends with the physician who treated me.

Also at the rehab and with my mother's help, I had my first real shower in nearly three months, which ended up being a bittersweet experience:

> Finally, I get to wash my hair, or at least what's left of it... the nurse at the other hospital did a fine job of detangling it, but yanked half of it off in the process. Anyway, I'm about to take my first shower in over two months, and I'm so excited I don't know what to do with myself. Not much of a choice there anyway, right? Someone transfers me (that's the word they like to use for moving patients who can't do so themselves from one place to another, such as from the bed to a chair) to a funky waterproof wheelchair with a seat that

> looks like a toilet. Apparently, they're known as shower wheelchairs. My mother wheels me down the hallway through the number coded doors. She's pretty surprised that I learned all the codes to get to the corridor where the showers were located just by watching the nurses punch them in. *I'm not brain dead, mom.* Once there, she pulls my gown off for the festivities.
>
> The pouring water is like tiny cotton pellets of heaven on my skin. This is the best shower ever. Or at least that's what it feels like right now. Simultaneously, though, I start to think of what this all means; my mother having to shampoo my hair as I sit practically motionless in a wheelchair, unable to do anything *myself.* Suddenly I start to sob uncontrollably and become inconsolable. Is this some kind of cosmic joke? *Why God??? Did you have to take this moment away too?!! Has my life really come to this...?* What a miserable existence; I hate life.

Evidently, that was one of the times I felt like I had gotten royally screwed. The low points for me were much more prevalent than the high points, and that was one of the lower ones. Looking back, I can understand how going through any hardship, can cause defeatist feelings to come into play. I've been there. I even get what it's like to be in that dark place for a really long time. The object, though, is to avoid getting stuck there, because that's how you miss the bigger picture. Hindsight is 20/20, so most often you won't even be able to look at things objectively until after the storm has passed. But once it has, why continue to dwell on it? As the Buddhist saying goes, "Living in the past is depression…"

In contrast to the shower episode, I do have some fun anecdotes from my stay at the rehab center. For example, the patients on my wing were all sitting around the breakfast table one morning before our daily grind began. One of the other patients, an older woman, asked for a cup of tea.

> She has a full coffee in front of her, now she wants tea? Wow, I am the youngest person at this table by far. How I long for home… Wait a minute! She's dunking her tea bag in her coffee. Hahahahahahah that's kind of funny. Woah! why am I laughing like that was the most hysterical thing in the world? It wasn't that funny. People are starting to stare in my direction.

Earth, please swallow me!

That was my first encounter with what I later found out is called pseudo-bulbar affect (PBA), which causes inappropriate and/or uncontrollable laughter or tears. Speaking of which, shortly after my return home a mass was held for me at a local church. It was sometime during the ceremony that my brother made me laugh (it was completely silly, he yanked me by the hand, which isn't funny) and I began laughing like a mad woman – meaning EXTREMELY LOUDLY. Thankfully I don't embarrass easily anymore. Afterwards, I had to apologize to the priest.

The other side of the coin is how incredibly blessed I feel to have my cognitive abilities intact, as that is not always the case for people who have suffered strokes. Can it be because I wasn't in a situation I felt the need to run away from, which a cognitive impairment would cause? Who knows - it's just something that I've occasionally wondered about. What I do know is that everything happens for a reason. And although it may not seem so at the time, it's there to serve us somehow. Things and events in themselves are neither good nor bad, they are neutral. We assign meaning to everything, and that involves choice. For example, you can react to a situation or you can respond to it, which basically means taking a few breaths when something unexpected happens in your life before doing or saying anything at all. When you finally do respond, you'll automatically be doing so from a higher place, instead of just reacting.

Not long ago, I heard of someone being described as an inverse paranoid - which I thought was brilliant. An inverse paranoid, you see, thinks that the world is conspiring to do him good in every situation. What an amazing outlook. The majority, if not all of us, thinks in the exact opposite way. Imagine the world of possibilities that would open up for us if we began to think like this. Have you heard of the saying that what you focus on expands? What would your life be like if you chose to only focus on the good in everything?

Meanwhile, due to insurance limits, I was released from the rehab center after two months. Despite the three hours of therapy five days a week in which I made steady progress, I left the rehab center in a wheelchair. Though I wasn't able to walk out, I had improved drastically. I had regained much of the mobility on the right side of my body, and was now able to eat regular food. So after my family learned how to transfer me from my wheelchair to my bed/vehicle, I finally got to go home. And how sweet it was; I had longed for my own bed for over three months and was overjoyed to sleep in it at long last. Silly as it sounds in the scope of things, it's probably one of the things I looked forward to the most.

My first challenge (and at the same time blessing) was that my wheelchair didn't fit through the doorways in my apartment. That was the instant I graduated to using a walker (only in the house at the beginning). Think about that for a moment. I couldn't move about in the wheelchair at home, so I decided I had to use a walker instead – As Plato once said, necessity really is the mother of all invention. Although it was awfully difficult at first, it gradually became easier and easier. The important word to take note of here is *decided*. When you make a decision to do something and really commit to it, it's basically a done deal. There's a great saying by William Hutchinson Murray that states "the moment one definitely commits oneself, then Providence moves too." The quote is much longer, and very powerful. It's about being truly committed to an outcome, and how this seemingly causes things to just naturally fall into place. The power of the mind amazes me more and more as I go further down the rabbit hole and learn about what we're truly capable of.

I then realized that it was inevitable that I would draw attention wherever I went. After all, I was in my mid 20s and in a wheelchair, which in and of itself sparks curiosity. But not really being able to speak coupled with the fact that my eyes were now totally misaligned (the stroke affected my left eye muscles, weakening them so that I became cross-eyed and began to see double), drew a line of separation between me and others, giving me an almost extrinsic quality that made people assume I was cognitively impaired. Some people would speak to whoever I was with as if I wasn't even there. Others would talk loudly at me as if I had the comprehension of a half-deaf four year old. The issue with my eyes only became resolved after months of eye exercises that a specialist recommended. I also wore what's known as a prism on the left eye of my regular glasses for many months. This was a plastic lens on top of the glass lens that had ground-in vertical lines (prisms) that corrected my vision when wearing my glasses.

My brain and body were now operating on two different levels, and that led to one of my biggest struggles; feeling like I was being condescended to. My sense of self-worth was close to nonexistent, and my interactions with people - especially those I didn't already know - just added insult to injury. Oftentimes, I felt belittled and as though I was being talked down to. I understand no one was doing this consciously or purposely, but I nevertheless agonized over it and would play insignificant events over and over in my head. I no longer felt like I was being treated as an equal. Roman mentioned that he had similar feelings. He said he had a really difficult time pushing me around in the wheelchair and seeing people stare at me with pity in their eyes.

Having to wear diapers was another extremely bitter pill for me to swallow. Yes - you read that correctly - diapers. They're known as "adult" diapers, which I had no idea existed before any of this either. They are very different from the brand Depends, which is what probably came to mind, in that what I'm referring to are actual full-blown diapers but for grownups. Anyhow, I had very little control over my bladder and bowels. If I wasn't very close to a bathroom the second the need to use it hit, some sort of accident was guaranteed (a fact made more than clear on numerous occasions). It was the most bizarre experience. It was like going through infancy again, only this time being conscious of it and observing myself unable to control my own body, and at the total mercy of others. I mean, imagine a diaper change at 25 – the things that ran through my head and all the different emotions that arose. Humiliation was right up there at first. Then, it gradually morphed into a deep sense of gratitude and appreciation for the true meaning of compassion. Also on the positive side - due to things such as me falling down a good number of times in public and my issues with incontinence - my embarrassment threshold is extremely high now. I basically have no sense of shame anymore, which is really quite liberating – sort of like being drunk without drinking!

Now that I was home again, my family members all turned into a bunch of dictators by having me do therapy for almost entire days during the time before I started outpatient therapy. Heck, they even made me do it even after treatment began. I still remember how my brother turned into a drill-sergeant; one of the exercises I remember most vividly is the lunges he made me do as

I held on to the footboard of my bed for balance.

We also have a recumbent bike that they forced me to ride. At first, I didn't have the strength to pedal - my feet would slip right off. My ever-so resourceful family found a solution to that little challenge though – they took a rope and tied my feet fast to the pedals until I regained enough strength to keep my feet on without help. And although I was pretty resentful at the time because of everything they were putting me through, today I can't thank them enough. I am amazed and truly grateful for the way they dedicated themselves to my rehabilitation. I wouldn't and couldn't have done it without them. They provided me with the motivation and even the willpower I no longer had inside myself.

Before starting outpatient therapy, I received therapy at home for some time from a young gentleman. I credit him with getting my left arm moving again. I still have an image of him holding it up against the wall while I sat on the couch. I really appreciate all he and every therapist I've been lucky enough to work with did for me. They've all been really dedicated to me and to making this bumpy road easier to navigate.

Months later, once I was potty trained (there is something inherently wrong with that statement when referring to an adult…), I began outpatient therapy at the same facility where I had spent two months as an inpatient. My family's quest for *my* recovery had begun long before though, and I say my family's because they seemed to have as much vested in it as I did, if not more. Remembering it today, I'd say it was even more because I was already past the breaking point. They were the ones that held on to the vision of me being healthy again, whereas I was ready to just throw in the towel.

After having been at home again for a while, my brother decided to take me to the pool. In reality, it wasn't so much for the therapeutic effects, but more for the fun of it. Much to my dismay though, I sunk like a ton of bricks as soon as I got in the water.

> Oh yes, finally somewhere where my physical condition won't be so apparent to me. I'll swim a few laps and have some fun. I can forget about everything for a bit and just relax. The water is a little warm but it feels great on my skin. Finally, my entire body is immersed, so here goes nothing…! Wait a second, am I really sinking??? Holy s*^#! This can't be. I try to advance in the water over and over, but to no avail. Finally, resigned and totally defeated, I break into loud sobs. "No, don't try to comfort me!" I scream at everyone who's rushing towards me. But it ends up sounding like a loud, breathy and barely intelligible whisper, which adds even more wood to the fire. God, if you're

actually up there, why didn't you just let me die???

Frustration and dismay engulfed me in a blanket of darkness. I felt as if the weight of the world was on my shoulders. *Is this what the rest of my life is going to be like???* I was pissed at the world, resentful that others could do what I no longer could... I had drawn the short end of the stick and now I was being unjustly punished for it. I seriously questioned the whole point of living life with this constant feeling of anguish. As time went on, constantly feeling dismay became a bit of a norm for me. Something would set me off and I'd go on a downward spiral until something I perceived as good happened again - and believe me, I was a tough audience. As the months and years passed, those feelings became less extreme.

Fortunately, one of the lifeguards at the pool took a special interest in me, and decided to work with me over many months. Today, I'm a pretty good swimmer, much better than I was before. It's another one of the things that's been immensely beneficial to my recovery.

While I was making progress with the physical therapy at the hospital, it seemed like things were only moving at a snail's pace. Somewhere along the way, I heard of hyperbaric therapy for brain injuries and began researching the topic. It involves a sealed and pressurized chamber, where patients enter and breathe pure oxygen which increases the amount of oxygen in the blood. It got pretty inconclusive reviews overall; some positive some negative. But I was pretty desperate, so I decided to go to Germany for five weeks of rehab, to a clinic where patients got oxygen therapy daily.

With the help of friends I had made while in Munich, I registered at a clinic in Schwarzwald, near Stuttgart, Germany. Traveling alone was not an option at the time, so my mother came with me. Overall, the trip ended up making me much healthier. It was a whole program, rather than just oxygen therapy. I had a full and varied schedule each day that included different treatments and therapies, the likes of which I hadn't seen in the US. One therapist even had me playing tennis (at a time when my balance was terrible), and hiking in the forest where the clinic was located. The center is, by the way, one that only uses natural medicine, which played a big role in me later taking an interest in naturopathy. And I was able to communicate in German, which was fantastic!

When I returned to the States, people commented on how much better I was doing. The hyperbaric therapy had notably improved my speech. I don't understand the mechanics of it, I'm just happy that it did. Although my stroke did not actually affect the language center in my brain, it did completely wreck the area responsible for coordination of any kind. That translated into not being able to coordinate my breath, voice, and all other organs and body parts that have anything to do with speech formation, a condition which is known as apraxia. I know exactly what I want to say, but there is a disruption in the part of the brain that sends the signal to the muscle for the corresponding specific movements. Somehow, the coordination of the speech muscles improved, though I still live with some of the effects of apraxia today.

My speech has actually been one of my biggest hang-ups. I'd often look at others in similar situations, but who could still speak normally, and I would think to myself – I'd trade a paralyzed arm to have normal speech. And I'm certain many of them thought the same about me, that they would love to be in my situation and be able to move both arms but have a slight speech problem. The grass always seems greener on the other side, doesn't it? Believe me, it really isn't.

Today, I no longer have such a limited mentality; I work on expanding it through inner work each day. The way I see it now is that I'm blessed to have full function of my limbs, *and* my speech is constantly improving. I don't look at it as being an either or thing anymore. The universe is limitless; the possibilities are infinite. If you can imagine it, it can be yours, whatever it is. You and I are much more powerful than we can ever imagine.

Chelation therapy was my next venture on the road to recovery. A relative living in Madrid (the cousin who played tour guide for us when we went to the embassy during my childhood) is an osteopath, which is someone who practices a form of alternative healthcare. He organized an appointment for me to go see a doctor friend of his who had become a naturopath and would administer the therapy. Chelation involves administering chelation agents intravenously to remove heavy metals from the body. Basically the fluids run throughout your veins, dragging the metals with them into the kidneys, until you are ready to go get rid of them by urinating. I did this for about three or four months three days a week. Since the treatment protocol would last a minimum of three months, my cousin found a place for my mother and I to rent.

Some weeks after the start of treatment, and upon the doctor's recommendation, my mother went to our home town in the north. I was now living alone for the first time since I'd had the stroke, which was really overwhelming at first. My second childhood suddenly came to a halt. I now had to figure things out for myself, like what groceries to buy for the week, what to cook, when to clean, and all the other things adults do. Yet at the same time it was very freeing. Being forced to fend for myself not only did wonders for me physically, but mentally as well. I lived alone in the apartment for about four months. After about seven months total, we were back in the States. My self-confidence was up, and I was doing better both physically, and especially emotionally.

It was in Spain that I discovered I could still ride a bicycle, in spite of my less than stellar balance; I guess the saying is true – you never forget how to ride one.

> This is going to be interesting. Yoli loaned Oscar and I her brother's bike. She must not care for it much... Anyway, we're at the park on a smooth court so I jump on it as Oscar holds it in place. He tells me to start pedaling and with one hand on the handle bar and one on the seat, he walks alongside of me for some time. But suddenly – What the hell is he doing? "Are you nuts?! Don't let go of me like that! I'm going to crack my head open...!" But wait a minute, I didn't fall right off! Is this really happening?

Despite the few close calls, I was actually riding on my own. I was gaining confidence in my ability as the minutes passed and was able to ride the bike for longer distances. As soon as I realized what was happening, I broke down and spent a lot of the afternoon crying, but this time they were tears of joy. I felt a lightness in my soul the likes of which I couldn't remember – at that very moment, the future started looking much brighter.

Back in New Jersey, I got the news that my best friend was going to get married in the coming months, and in Latin America! So my next trip was to Ecuador during the wedding planning stages. My mother came as well, though she stayed with some family friends while I stayed with Maria and her fiancé. I did spend a few days with my mom and her friends, though, who thought to take me to an alternative medicine and homeopathic center in Quito.

The doctor I saw was amazing. He recommended stem cell injections for me. I didn't know the first thing about this type of treatment, but decided to go ahead and try it. Unfortunately, I wouldn't be able to start the treatment until a few months later, since the medication had to be prepared in Europe, shipped to Ecuador, and then brought (not shipped) to me in the States (which my mom's friends offered to do on one of their trips to the U.S. to visit family). Isn't it amazing how things just tend to work themselves out?

Since the injections were intra muscular, I had other people inject them into my upper thigh, because I was too squeamish to do it myself. At first, a nurse who is friends with someone my mother knows, gave me the injections. Later I had my brother do it. Did they work? I'll answer that the same way I do when people ask in person. I did so many things, and was doing so many of them at the same time, that it's difficult to pinpoint what worked and what didn't. I've been recovering for literally nine plus years; to this day, it's an ongoing process. And I especially find it hard to evaluate myself because it's been so gradual, that it's difficult to make judgments on a day-to-day basis. It's easier for people who don't see me often to notice improvements. Yet at the same time, I know these have been steady. Something worked – the synergy of all things together? Or was it the belief that I was going to recover that brought all these things into my experience in the first place?

Stem cell injections were the last of my unorthodox treatment methods. Other than the things I've already mentioned, I experimented, and continue to experiment, with my diet. Right now I'm mostly vegetarian. The correct term would be pescetarian because I do eat fish, and on rare occasions I'll enjoy beef or chicken if it's organic. That also goes for vegetables – I buy organic when possible, though I'm not hell bent on *only* organics when it comes to veggies. I don't doubt there are benefits to consuming only organic products, especially when dealing with specific health issues/concerns. I just find it too restrictive and since I'm a foodie, I won't do it.

Along the way, I also joined a local gym so I could continue my rehabilitation and decided to give yoga class a shot, and I haven't looked back since. I was immediately hooked. It wasn't too strenuous or quick paced, and the poses could easily be modified to fit my physical condition. At the same time, I was getting stronger.

I credit my yoga practice with my calmness, serenity, and peace of mind. My whole demeanor changed in what I consider a fairly short amount of time. I became more positive and stopped pushing so hard against everything – I learned to flow. I couldn't pinpoint what brought on this attitude change at first, but now I know that not only is yoga physically strengthening, it's also a very powerful mental exercise. As the story goes, yoga was actually developed to facilitate meditation, which is something I would eventually start practicing as well. I also started doing other mind/body work as a result. The best case I can make for practicing yoga is that after his first yoga class, someone I know who's going through a very difficult situation told me that "that was the first time in three weeks that my mind was quiet."

What I call my first step back into the real world was my return to school. I tested into a two year long continuing education program in Spanish to English translation. I mention the testing aspect because I suffered a complete lack of confidence in myself and didn't think I'd pass the entrance exam, which was timed but online. I was somewhat surprised and in sheer joy when I got the news that I was accepted. For the most part, the program itself was also online, though I did end up taking one course on campus. That course ended up being a stepping stone for me as well, since it was my first interaction with a group of people outside of physical therapy.

In retrospect, I see the experience as being a positive one; though I didn't quite see it that way at the time.

Back then, I was basically living in my own head and the negative feedback in the form of incessant chatter was overwhelming. I would hear things like "You limp. Everyone will wonder what happened. You don't sound like everyone else. People will think you're stupid if you talk…" (and other such pleasantries). I am happy to say that despite that not quite so little voice, I made it a point to attend every class and asked questions whenever I felt lost. To this day, I still hear that voice. The big difference, though, is in the volume; the critic squatting in my head (or my roommate, as I more lovingly refer to it) will probably never totally disappear, and that's not even what I strive for. I'm thrilled at being able to acknowledge the voice, and move forward anyway. It doesn't have the paralyzing force over me it once had. I attribute its taming – again – to yoga (meditation came later).

My next venture was volunteering at a radio station. Though it seems pretty unrelated to translation, it was just the next logical step for me. How I stumbled upon this appears accidental enough: I use a radio alarm clock, and one morning when my alarm went off, a station that I never even knew existed came on. My nephew, who was probably three or four at the time, must have been playing with it the day before. Anyhow, the voices were slightly distorted because the frequency was off a bit, but I could hear the commentator talking about a conspiracy theory regarding the 9/11 attacks, and all I could think was "Holy crap!!! Am I actually hearing this? Is this really being broadcasted on an FM radio station??? How bold!" I was really impressed, so I found out where the station was located, went there armed with a resume, and offered to volunteer a few days a week. They accepted and I was thrilled!

Since I didn't have the pressure of having to make ends meet, I was able to enjoy the luxury of volunteer work. And I consider it a luxury, because nowadays, people are too busy to even handle the things on their own plates. I was very fortunate in this regard because apparently, when I filled out my medical insurance papers at my last corporate job, I chose a long term insurance policy. And I say "apparently" because at the age of 25, there is no way I would have consciously opted into it. The only way I can explain it is that it must have read something like "sign here to opt out," and I just overlooked it. So not only had I been receiving social security disability payments, but I also have this monthly income which pays more on top of it. Not to mention, my mother moved into my apartment, and we rented the other floor. So in addition to everything else they have done for me, my parents have also been a big help financially. Was the insurance thing a coincidence? I don't believe in coincidences. In my mind, things happen the way they do for a reason. Although the reasons for my life unfolding the way that it has are not totally clear to me yet, I sense that I have greater purpose, and I believe that writing this book is just the beginning of it.

To get back to the radio station, it was listener sponsored and had no advertisements; for revenue, they hold quarterly fund drives and offer different products for pledges or donations. I tuned in during one of these drives one day and was really interested in the product being offered. It was a CD series – Your Wish is Your Command by Kevin Trudeau. In a nutshell, Kevin was saying that you create your life and can manifest whatever you like. Since I'd never heard such things before, it sounded a bit far-fetched; like pie-in-the-sky. Manifesting? Interesting concept, but was that all it was; a concept? My curiosity was peaked, though, so I kept listening. I ended up pledging to get the set. It wasn't until a few months later that it arrived, but I immediately started to play it when it finally did.

PART III

Awakening

Everything I heard on those CDs was radically different from anything I'd ever heard before, from everything that had been ingrained in me throughout my life. The logical thing would have been to stop listening, but for some reason, it resonated with me. And after I listened to the whole series all the way through, I began playing it over and over, so much so that I must have heard it from beginning to end at least fifty times.

One of the CDs in the set of twelve is dedicated to improving how you feel at every moment. *Was feeling good really as important as Kevin made it out to be?* He also mentions Thought Field Therapy (TFT) as a way to boost your mood by getting rid of negative emotions instantly. TFT is a unique form of energy healing that focuses on the emotional body. It's actually the parent of EFT (Emotional Freedom Technique). I enrolled in a weekend course taught by Joanne Callahan, who is the wife of the man who invented the technique.

I started playing with other concepts as well, such as manifestation. It took me a while to actually see evidence of it working, but when I finally did, I was in complete awe. The very first thing I manifested was communication from an old friend in Spain, someone I see maybe once every two years or so, and with the exception of these sporadic meetings, do not communicate with at all. When I finally got an email from her a few months later, I was pretty shocked, but it was still easy for me to chalk it up to coincidence.

One of my next manifestations was a two dollar bill. It just showed up by popping out of a friend's wallet as we were paying for lunch early one afternoon. I nearly leapt out of my seat with excitement and began to laugh nervously. I was too amazed to even tell her why I was so exhilarated for about five minutes. Could this have been yet another coincidence??

It was at this time that a friend of mine named Kevin invited me to the Ormus Conference in Hiawassee, Georgia. He was one of the vendors, and said that he could use my help. I had the time, so I jumped at the opportunity. The conference was very interesting; it was about a topic of which I hadn't heard before – Ormus. Without delving into it too deeply, it is a group of substances exhibiting many miraculous properties, such as healing powers and superconductivity at room temperature. In a nutshell, Ormus is often referred to as the "biblical manna," "white powder of gold," and even the "Philosopher's Stone."

Anyhow, the resort owner had prepared a special treat for the attendees one evening; it was a program called "Living Without Limits." I had no clue what to expect but I was interested in seeing what it was all about, especially because I knew it was interactive and caught sight of some of the things which were in store for the participants. *Heck no, there's no way on God's green earth I'm doing that, but I'm sure as hell curious to see what happens.* Also, the organizers were pretty adamant when they said that we were in for an extraordinary experience.

And was it ever extraordinary. It's really what got the ball rolling on personal growth for me. The gist of the evening's message was basically that we have these self-imposed limitations, when in reality we are limitless. We participated in a series of exercises that really drove the point home, which I won't disclose because the company still runs programs out of Florida. Check them out if you have the chance to, they're truly more astounding and inspiring than words can express. What I can say is that there was one particular challenge that, in spite of three attempts, I was not able to surpass. Then one of the organizers said he'd stay with me all night if that's what it took for me to do it (after the event was over).

When it was all said and done, a few of the other

participants and I returned to the main hall. Despite a few more painful tries, I was still not able to conquer the challenge. Chik - the organizer - used some EFT on me (it's an offspring of TFT and stands for Emotional Freedom Technique – a form of psychological acupressure, based on the same energy meridians used in traditional acupuncture to treat physical and emotional ailments) and the waterworks began. With tears rolling down my face and my emotions running so high, I began talking about how I felt inadequate, less than, disabled… And voila! On the next try, I was successful. When I realized what had happened, I literally began wailing like a banshee – it was a mixture of release, pure joy, empowerment, excitement, and a bag of other high-flying emotions. Some of the people that stuck around who are sensitive to energies said I released a wave of it that reverberated throughout the room. I didn't get to bed until 2 or 3 am, though it didn't matter because I wasn't able to sleep the entire night. I lay awake thinking about the endless possibilities that lay ahead.

Upon returning home, I bought many books on the topic of personal development and became an avid reader. First, I purchased all the books Mr. Trudeau recommends in his CD series. And that's how I stumbled upon Abraham-Hicks. Shortly thereafter, someone I had met at the conference in Georgia gave me a large quantity of audio books and recordings of Hicks' seminars, which I listen to often. Their message resonates with me so much that I went to one of their live seminars in LA. Since they hold seminars all over the country, LA seems like a long way to go for a one day event – but, of course, there's a story there.

In conversation with Kevin (from the Ormus conference), I found out that he was supposed to go see the Hick seminar in LA. Unfortunately something had come up and he wouldn't be able to go. He asked if I would be willing to take his ticket. Initially I felt that it was too far and hesitated. But he ended up connecting me with the woman from LA who he was supposed to go with, and she offered me a room in her house. Even though the ticket turned out to be non-transferable, I figured heck, I've never been to California and I have a place to stay, so why not?

Since I'd never been to the West coast, I booked a trip for approximately ten days. The first few days, I stayed with Kevin's friend and had a fantastic time. The rest of the time, I stayed at a hotel with someone else's points. It so happens that the tenant upstairs has a friend who gets thousands of them at the Marriott, and he very graciously allowed me to use some of them. So basically, I only paid my car rental for the latter part of the trip. Magic, huh?

Kevin's friend, Cyrene, introduced me to the "game" of manifesting. The way it worked was that she and some friends would decide on an object, and whoever brought it into their experience first won the round. I thought it was clever and started doing the same thing with a friend who's on a similar path once I was back in NJ. It was more entertaining than playing alone, as I had been doing until then. Some of the objects manifested were a blimp, a white bunny, and a tandem bike, among others. Try it – it's fun and very empowering. When the "object" appears before me, no matter how many times I play, a light turns on inside me. And then I am overwhelmed with a feeling of gratitude and renewed confidence about life. The object of the game is to continually manifest things you perceive as more challenging, and thereby strengthen your focus and manifesting muscles. The reality is that it's as easy to manifest a button as it is a castle, but our self-limiting beliefs get in the way.

At the Abraham-Hicks seminar, I met someone who invited me to an Abraham gathering at his beach front home (organized through www.meetup.com). There I met someone who later put me in contact with the people I would later volunteer for after leaving the radio station. Since my core personality was starting to change, I was no longer attracted to that heavy type of environment, and when I got back to New York, I instead ended up editing audio books as an intern for the library of Congress.

On this trip, I also met two other huge Abraham fans (who were friends with Cyrene) and became Facebook friends with them. Not long after coming back to New Jersey, I saw a post from one of them on my news feed about a Robert Kiyosaki seminar. I knew of Kiyosaki because I had very recently purchased his book Rich Dad, Poor Dad, though I hadn't gotten around to reading it yet. So I did some research and found out that one of these seminars was taking place in New York in the coming weeks, which I naturally went to check out. While I was there, I signed up for a three day seminar to be held a few months later. The seminar was really enlightening, and at the end of it I signed up for a junior package on real estate education.

When my first class came around in the summer, I met a dear man, who gave me a free ticket to another three day seminar. I was curious and asked him about it, to which his only reply was "You'll like it!" I must have been satisfied with that extremely vague answer because I signed up for the next one which was going to be held in New Jersey in April of the following year. When I think about it now, I still don't understand why I agreed to go. I mean, even the title – Millionaire Mind Intensive (by T. Harv Eker) – was somewhat of a turnoff for me. And here I was, taking the word of a stranger about how I'd like it. And, not only did I sign up, but I paid for an upgrade!

April finally rolled around, and frankly, I was delightfully surprised by the seminar! Despite the long hours, I had an amazing weekend; so much so that I felt a sort of melancholy when it ended on Sunday afternoon. In keeping with the company's tradition, I won't disclose what goes on at this three-day course. Besides, I wouldn't even be able to find the right words. It's one of those things one needs to experience for themselves. If you've been to one before, you know what I'm talking about. And if you haven't, I highly recommend looking into it.

One of the biggest lessons I took away from the seminar that weekend was the jar system, which is a fantastic money management system. I implemented it immediately. At first it was a stretch for me, particularly the jar known as the PLAY jar – which is where 10% of your income goes (and you then get to blow every month!). Since I am a saver, almost to the point of hoarding money, I made the play jar a whopping 12%. At the beginning I found this spending to be frivolous and had a difficult time deciding what to do with the money. Now I look forward to it every month! This allows more prosperity and abundance to flow into my life. The number one wealth principle states "Treat yourself like a precious object, for it will make you strong." When I first heard that, it held little meaning for me. Now I'm beginning to understand the importance of feeling worthy, and in creating your dream life. To learn more about the jar system, you can quickly do a Google search for the terms "jar system"+ "T. Harv Eker."

At the MMI, I signed up for a stock trading course

which was taking place in Florida that July. When I went to it, I had the opportunity to speak to some of the Karma Krew members. These are the people that volunteer their time to make sure these events run smoothly. Again, they're not on staff, and travel on their own dime to be a part of these seminars. I liked what I heard and joined the Karma Krew as well.

My first event as a Krew member was an MMI in Charlotte, NC. I had such an amazing time. At one point, I even began to cry uncontrollably for no apparent reason. I believe I was overwhelmed by the love I felt; it was so pure, so unconditional. I just felt at home. At that event, I won another Peak Potentials course and decided to go to their Warrior Camp the following August in BC, Canada.

A few months later, I participated as a Krew member at another MMI, this time in New Jersey. And wouldn't you know it? I won another course, making it two in a row!! Now that's what I call being on fire...! While on the Krew, I met some really supportive, genuine people. One of the other Krew members, Carmen, actually later became one of my good friends. Something she said to me then made me decide to sign up for a Warrior Camp being held in California in January. I wanted to wait until August, mostly because of the location and partly because of my "lack mentality" that told me it was too much travel in a short period of time. I mean, I had just returned from Florida in July and North Carolina in October. Mind you, it's not like I have a job to worry about. I just have a tendency to stockpile money (for lack of a better word), which is something I work on improving every day. Thank you for the jar system Harv! Anyhow, her statement was about not waiting for the better location if I was committed to going to the camp, so I went.

The camp was so amazing, it just blew my mind. I'm sworn to secrecy on the what went on, but what I can say is that going through it made me feel a calm decisiveness about how to proceed with my life – in the sense of moving forward with much more certainty. Another big lesson I learned was that it's not so much about making the right choice or not, as long as you make *a* choice. Additionally, the boost to my self-confidence was tremendous; and self-confidence is at the base of - and heavily impacts - anything and everything you do. There is a quote by Marcus Tullius Cicero that sums it up nicely, "if you have no confidence in self, you are twice defeated in the race of life. With confidence, you have won even before you have started." More on this later…

Around this time, Carmen, and I became closer friends. It's so true that like attracts like, for we are similar in many ways. Anyhow, she'd be attending another Peak Potentials seminar in early March of that year in California, which I decided to attend also. It was a stretch for me, since I'd just returned from the West

Coast at the beginning of February, but that's what it's all about; breaking through your comfort zone, because that's where everything you want is.

The seminar, Master of Influence, was a multi-speaker event, and the orators were brilliant. The most profound and valuable lesson I left with is that influence is not about converting others to your way of thinking, but rather about being so sure of yourself and who you are that others are naturally attracted to you. Is the message here clear? Self-confidence is one of the most important building blocks for all achievement. It's part of the foundation for having abundant success in all areas of your life. It makes sense if you think about it; confidence follows success. If you have confidence, you are that much more likely to go the extra distance and push through temporary set-backs (that's how Napoleon Hill refers to what we commonly consider failures in Think and Grow Rich). In reality, there is no such thing as failure; rather it's temporary in nature, and necessary for all future achievement. It's important to recognize this so that you can make corrections and continue pushing forward. The object is not to quit. Did you know that the Apollo 13 (the first rocket to the moon) was only on course 3% of the time? Remember that next time you hit a snag or bump on the road, and keep moving forward in total confidence.

In the meantime, I've been volunteering at more Peak Potential events. These have been MMI's in both

New Jersey and North Carolina. And I recently returned from participating in Wizard Training Camp in BC, Canada, which is the follow-up to Warrior Camp. Whereas in Warrior the focus was on pushing through obstacles, this Wizard Training was more about avoiding them all together - which has a whole lot to do with your perspective.

Actually, at the end of the day, perspective is what everything really boils down to. The following story from my trip to the camp illustrates this perfectly:

On my way to Vancouver, I surprisingly ended up missing both legs of my flight. Since I was up and about by 4 am that morning, I thought I had plenty of time to catch the first plane. Fate thought otherwise though. First off, since I was storing a friend's vehicle while he was away (and it just so happens that I flew out the day he returned), I planned to park the car in a lot near the airport for him. It was all set up and ready to go with an online reservation he had made. But when I went to drop the car off, I found out that it was not valet parking and I would have had to take the keys with me, so I had to go to a different lot. Then, for some strange reason, I got confused about the airline I was on and went to the wrong terminal. Yet it took me and the attendant at least 15 minutes to realize that I was at the wrong counter! When we finally figured it out, I made my way to the other terminal and was finally able to get a boarding pass. But the flight left from the terminal I had just come from! Now would be a good time to mention that I'm not the speediest person in the world. Anyhow, I started to make my way back, when I suddenly noticed that my boarding pass said that I was on a later flight. I got alarmed because I was originally connecting in Phoenix and wasn't sure I'd make it anymore. So I went back to the person who helped me. Her response was that my flight had been switched and I was now on a later - but direct - flight to Vancouver. So I thought "great, this is turning out pretty well!" I started to walk back to the terminal where I had originally started, as briskly as possible this time because now I was pressed for time.

When I was just about to get on the Air tram, I looked at the boarding pass I was holding only to realize that it had the incorrect (first) name on it!!! I couldn't believe my eyes, which started to burn as I held back tears of rage. I returned to the person that had been helping me all along, and after ten minutes she figured out that I was at the wrong airline! It was bizarre! I finally made my way to the correct counter, only to find out I had missed the first leg of my flight, and therefore the second one as well, because there were no flights to Phoenix that arrived in time to make the Vancouver flight.

So now it was 6:30 in the morning, and the next flight to Arizona was not until a bit after nine - which was fine, except for the fact that I had a seven hour layover ahead of me in Phoenix. As I thought about this,

I could feel myself getting more and more irritated. But then I had another thought, *What if this is happening for a reason? Maybe I'm being kept from something negative or perhaps there's someone I'm supposed to meet.* That immediately calmed me down and just as quickly shifted the whole situation for me. Shortly thereafter, I met a man who offered to take me to the first class lounge with his membership card when we got to Phoenix. I thought "Woo hoo! That's pretty cool." Then something just as cool happened; I got upgraded to first class! So it turned out to be quite the trip. I rode to the airport in style in my friend's red convertible BMW, flew first class on both legs of the trip, and sat in the executive lounge during my layover.

My ensuing experience at Wizard Training Camp was, to say the least, phenomenal! The biggest lesson I took away from it is that there's no reason for me to hide. See, I'd been feeling terribly insecure and inadequate after my brain injury, and I had been making myself as invisible as possible to others. To be honest, I've always had what I would call social issues. To say these were self-esteem issues, though, would be somewhat inaccurate. I was taught to blend with the crowd, to not stand out. And post-injury, wanting to blend in or be invisible was a constant thought in my mind, which really then became about self-esteem. I liked to blame my subtle limp and my breathy, sometimes raspy voice. But I even see these things differently now. Whenever people ask me if I lost my voice, I just reply "Nope, my voice is just that sexy (or something similar)." That immediately neutralizes the situation for me while at the same time creating a light and playful environment.

I am also learning to accept my victories, regardless of the shape they take. However, being a perfectionist (which I trace back all the way to the school incident when I was a child, along with other events that paved this road called life) and having to deal with certain physical issues is no easy task. There have been times, such as at Wizard Camp, where I did not meet certain challenges on my own. My conditioned mind immediately wanted to rob me of the victory by discounting whatever I might have accomplished because I had help. I'm learning to let go of that mentality and to not be so attached to the self-limiting "perception" of those victories. When the same end result is achieved, does it make a difference if you did it alone or not? That has probably been another one of my biggest lessons along the way too; learning to accept help. Actually, having gone from an independent free spirit to total helplessness - which meant relying on others at every waking moment - has been the greatest lesson of all.

And the personal growth continues. I was recently at another Peak Potentials event, and - as always - they over-delivered. It was all about passive income and not exchanging your time for money. What a concept, right? – working because you want to, not because you have to. Think of all the things you'd be able to do. The majority of us are stuck on a hamster wheel, chasing a paycheck, and never doing the things we really love. Why? Because we think that's how life works; that that's how we get ahead. But the exact opposite is true. As Howard Thurman - the author, philosopher, theologian, educator and civil rights leader - put it, "Don't ask what the world needs. Ask what makes you come alive and go do it, because what the world needs is people who have come alive."

Not long after the course, I took part in another course called Sacred Gifts, which I was introduced to by another Peak Potentials student, Barbara. The gist of the course is that we are all born with certain gifts, or certain traits, that we wouldn't normally think of as gifts (the majority of them) and we can use these to live more fulfilling lives, while serving others. For more information, go to http://www.yoursacredgifts.com.

With what I learned about myself in this course, I am exploring life, and finding out what's a good fit for the new version of me. I also understand people better and why they behave the way they do as a result. The course was particularly eye opening in that I now understand where my strengths lie. I will look to develop those gifts in a way that will serve humanity, because that's what we're really all here for – to somehow be of service to others.

That is my intention. And to embrace the second chance at life I've been given as the new and improved Maria!

I hope my story has inspired you. Or at the very least helped you recognize that your worst tragedy may very well be the beginning of great things to come. Learn to look at it that way and it will become just that and more. It may seem hopeless right now, but your vision is narrow. In time you'll come to understand; just accept your circumstances with grace and know in your heart of hearts that there is indeed a reason for everything you are experiencing. And that reason will ultimately be beneficial for you in some way. As Alan Cohen so masterfully puts it, "every minus is a half of a plus, waiting for a stroke of vertical awareness."

PART IV

Pearls

My life has dramatically improved since becoming aware of – in addition to actively studying and applying - some of the principles of the Law of Attraction. So much so, that I felt compelled to put together the ones that have had the greatest impact in my own life. If you're not new to this Law, these will probably be largely familiar to you, as none of this information is originally mine. Nonetheless, I find it helpful to review the same material in different words, and you might too.

I consider the following to be my top ten pillars of success. Don't simply take my word for it, though. Try some of these (or all of them!) on for size in your own life. And if they do nothing for you, just throw them away.

[1] As Wayne Dyer often says, "Change the way you look at things, and the things you look at will change."

Earlier I mentioned that if you change your beliefs, your life will change. I know what you're thinking – "how the [bleep] can I change my beliefs?!" That's a question I constantly asked myself and am disappointed to find that no matter how much I read on the topic of personal development, that question is never really directly addressed. I believe the answer is by a life-long commitment to personal growth and to expanding your consciousness. For me that means reading and/or listening to audios on a daily basis, and attending seminars as often as I can. If you have financial concerns, use libraries, buy used books. There is also free stuff all over the internet.

Find a personal growth seminar being held near you, and then volunteer for it. Do this often. I can't stress the importance of being in that high energy environment enough. Because what good is it to attend a seminar, just to go back home, and do the exact same thing with the exact same people afterward? You would have increased your vibration temporarily, but the real goal is lasting change. For that to happen, you must continually strive to raise your vibration. Here's some food for thought: Realism is only society's acceptable form of pessimism.

Some of you might be wondering, "What on earth does she mean by vibration? Let's back-track for a second; everything in this world is made out of the same thing - energy. Scientists studied the make-up of moon rock, only to find that it's created of the same atoms you and I are made of, the same atoms found in water and in anything else you can think of. And an atom is made of rapidly moving particles, or energy. In this sense, when I suggest raising your vibration, I mean raise the frequency or rate of vibration at which these particles move. Why you ask? Well the things we want, namely abundance in all areas of life, can all be found at these higher frequencies. And it's when your vibration matches the vibration of the things you want that they come into your life.

The reality is that we must *unlearn* many - if not most - of the things we've picked up throughout our lives, rather than *learn anew*. The only way to truly do this is to replace the acquired information with new information through the use of repetition (which really is the mother of all learning!). It's mostly how we acquired the detrimental beliefs of our environment and society - beliefs that keep us in constant resistance to obtaining all that we desire. Think of it almost as purging yourself of old beliefs and habits, and filling/brain-washing your mind with new ideas that will instead support you and your growth in moving toward a better life. Here's some more food for thought: Realism is really a socially acceptable form of pessimism.

I firmly believe that you must make a lifelong commitment to personal growth if you want lasting change to occur in your life. Oftentimes, people attend a seminar one time and then think to themselves, "Nothing happened, this is stupid." The real key to change, however, is shifting your paradigm, as Bob Proctor puts it. A paradigm of reality is what really controls a person, but on the subconscious level. And the only way to change one is through repetition. You feed your body every day, don't you? You must feed your mind in the same way. Spend half an hour to an hour a day on yourself, on reading or listening to audios. I still remember when I first watched the movie The Secret, but what brought it all together for me and made me truly passionate about personal development is Kevin Trudeau's Your Wish is Your Command audio. I listened to it religiously, over and over and over. From there I went on to other books and speakers, as well as seminars.

I had never gone to a seminar before mid-2012 and now I am travelling all over the continent to attend them. I get that not everyone has the means to do so because of time and/or money, but there is so much free or low-cost information to take advantage of out there in the form of videos, books, audios, things on the internet etc., and there are even free seminars. I've already mentioned the Millionaire Mind Intensive seminar run by Peak Potentials, which is a serious game changer for many people. On the final night, I left actually feeling dread that it was over.

It's easier to stay in that high energy of personal

development seminars when you are aware of and monitor your environment, and associate with people of like minds. It's said that one's income is equal to the average income of the five people he/she associates with the most. I have no idea how accurate that is – I find the comment compelling though. Just think about it for a while and look around you. Can you find some truth in it? I sure can.

Along with a lifelong commitment to growth, the other crucial key to the puzzle is to understand that there is no one to blame - nor is anyone else responsible - for anything that happens in your life but yourself, for you are the sole creator of your experience. Again, you create everything that happens in your life through vibration. What I'm saying here is that if you're stopped at a red light and someone hits your car from behind, you co-created that, which means that it's as much your responsibility as the person's that hit you. It's a difficult concept to wrap one's head around; it almost seems unfair. Yet at the same time, it's tremendously liberating to know you have that much control. And depending on the meaning you give to events in your life, it can be even more empowering. You have the power to spin every situation positively by thinking things such as "maybe the universe is trying to prevent me from going further on this road now to avoid some kind of accident, or there's someone I'm supposed to meet." Instead we curse our luck when things don't go as we think they should. Remember, nothing has meaning but the meaning you give it. When I first heard that phrase at the Millionaire Mind Intensive I found it to be so incredibly profound, yet so simple at the same time. There is no such thing as good or bad, it's all a matter of how you look at it.

[2] The popular saying goes "you've got to see It to believe it." Well, the exact opposite is true. Believe it and you will see it, as Wayne Dyer points out in his book *You'll See it When You Believe it*. Everything begins in the mind, but you must first believe – in other words you must have faith. According to Matthew 17:20 "...if you have faith the size of a mustard seed, you will say to this mountain, 'Move from here to there,' and it will move; and nothing will be impossible to you." I'm not talking about faith in the religious sense (despite the Biblical reference!). It can mean something as simple as putting your faith in the universe, and trusting that whatever is going on in your life is happening to serve you in some way, as I've already mentioned. It's difficult to look at things that way when you're facing major challenges, but taking a step back from the situation and changing your perspective about it not only makes it easier to handle whatever is going on, but the issue will resolve itself sooner, and the reason for the experience will eventually become clear to you, whether it's rather quickly or ten years down the line.

It's a bit of a bitter pill to swallow, I totally get that. If anyone had said anything to me remotely similar to what I just said about tragedies really being blessings in disguise when I was in the midst of my stroke or my years of recovery, I would have probably been offended. But today, I can honestly look back and see that it was just the beginning of great things to come, and it's very satisfying to finally be able to recognize that.

A beautiful story that illustrates the power of belief is that of the Australian Cliff Young. I first heard the story from Jack Canfield, and I find it so impressive and powerful that I'd like to share it:

Cliff was a farmer, who had always wanted to run an extreme long distance race. Finally, at the age of 61, he decided to enter one and fulfill his dream.

On the day of the race, he showed up wearing his overalls and work boots, while everyone else had the latest running gear. The others were shocked, so they began to question him on his qualifications. "Have you ever run a long distance race before?" "No," Cliff answered. "How about a half marathon?" "No," Cliff answered again. "A 10 kilometer race?" When Cliff said no to that as well, the next question was "So what makes you think you could run this race?" And he said "I am a farmer, I chase my sheep around all day. I don't have a tractor. And sometimes when the storm is coming in, me and my dog may be out running around for two or three days without sleep, so I think I can do this."

The organizers didn't even want to let him enter, but finally they did.

When everyone took off rather fast, Cliff ran slowly, doing what is now called the "Cliff Young shuffle." Being totally inexperienced, he didn't know that you're supposed to run for 16 hours and sleep for eight. He was so far behind everyone the first night that no one was awake to tell him to go to bed. And they were up and gone before he even got to them.

But on the fourth night while everyone slept, Cliff ran past them. He ended up running for five and a half days non-stop to break the old record by twelve hours. See, the other runners believed they had to sleep every night, but Cliff didn't have that belief. He just continued on and ended up ahead of them all.

I truly believe that part of the reason why I had such a miraculous recovery is because I didn't know that I wasn't supposed to recover. For a long time, I wasn't aware that stroke tends to cause paralysis on one side of the body. Ignorance really was bliss in my case. Think about the saying next time you watch the news, which is basically negative propaganda. I'm not making a case for walking around in total ignorance - but if it's something important to your experience, you will hear about it. Furthermore, getting wrapped up in all the negativity on TV is actually detrimental to your own life experience in that your negative feelings about what you are watching actually attract more of those same feelings in the form of situations in your own life which cause them.

As Niurka says, you don't believe what you see, you see what you believe. Belief really is one of the most powerful forces in life. By the same token, a belief is just a thought you keep thinking. So change your beliefs and watch your life change before your eyes.

[3] In life, you don't get what you want. You get what you believe you deserve. – Oprah

The statement is astonishingly congruent with life. It ties belief and self-worth together beautifully. Be confident enough to understand how magnificent and worthy you truly are, and that you deserve the best of everything in life. A healthy self-esteem is one of the strongest factors for success. For if you lack self-esteem or self-worth, which goes hand in hand with self-confidence, the road to achieving your dreams will prove a difficult, if not impossible, one. The most significant thing I can add here is not to anchor your confidence on externals, whether they be people or objects. Let it flow from the inside out, starting with your belief in yourself.

Recently, I heard Marshall Sylver - a master of attracting abundance in every area of life - say something, which was incredibly deep yet simple; he said that "your net worth is tied to your self-worth." And self-confidence, which stems from having a good sense of self-worth, is at the foundation of practically any and all achievement. Many people lack self-confidence, which ultimately leads to fear, mostly of criticism from others and of being ostracized. This keeps us playing small, and stops us from ever reaching beyond our comfort zone. And as T. Harv Eker says "Your Comfort Zone = Your Money Zone." We expand each and every time we go out of our comfort zones.

An example of this, although not directly tied to money, would be approaching someone you're interested in meeting, even though you're painfully shy or insecure. I actually did this to prove a point to myself not long ago. And to my surprise, I didn't feel nearly as nervous as I thought I would. In other words, the thought was much worse than the deed. As we were in the middle of conversation, I noticed that I was relatively calm. As I think about this more and more, I realize I can turn my confidence on at times. And I bet most people can too. The trick is to make the feeling permanent. This is where I apply the "fake it til you make it" philosophy. In other words, act more confident than you really are - which is what I'm referring to when I talk about turning the confidence on. Just continue to do this for longer periods each time and eventually you'll become that person.

I'm no self-confidence expert, but one key piece of advice of gotten on this subject is that compliments raise it. So aim for getting as many as possible, which is pretty easy for a woman; wear something which you wouldn't normally wear, accessorize, etc. I guess for a man it would be somewhat similar - shaving if he doesn't do so on a regular basis, dressing up, etc. Another powerful thing is to be really knowledgeable in something (in your line of work, for example). You'll feel really confident each time you speak about it.

[4] The power of the law of attraction lies in feeling good. It sounds too simple to be true, but it really is that easy. Are you familiar with the saying "*When it rains, it pours?*" When you're feeling good, only good things can come to you (and I'm guessing that's where you want your point of attraction to be). The opposite is also true; when you're feeling crummy, things that keep you feeling crummy occur in your life. But again, watch how you interpret things; if something which you perceive as being negative happens and you've been feeling good and sending out high vibrations, ask yourself if the event really is negative.

Some things are difficult, if not impossible, to feel good about. The best way to deal with them is to not give them attention. Watch a comedy, read a book, do anything that will cause the focus to shift to something different. Dwelling and wallowing in whatever is causing you grief will bring things into your life that will cause you to continue feeling the same way (hence, the importance of feeling good).

What I really mean is that, ideally, you want to

reach for a slightly better feeling, since it's very difficult to jump directly from grief to joy. Let's say you're depressed; feeling better may mean feeling guilt, which is only one next step above it. The goal is to be moving up on the emotional scale, which according to Abraham-Hicks is as follows:

1. Joy/Appreciation/Empowered/Freedom/Love
2. Passion
3. Enthusiasm/Eagerness/Happiness
4. Positive Expectation/Belief
5. Optimism
6. Hopefulness
7. Contentment
8. Boredom
9. Pessimism
10. Frustration/Irritation/Impatience
11. Overwhelment
12. Disappointment
13. Doubt
14. Worry
15. Blame
16. Discouragement
17. Anger
18. Revenge
19. Hatred/Rage
20. Jealousy
21. Insecurity/Guilt/Unworthiness
22. Fear/Grief/Depression/Despair/Powerlessness

Find where you are on the scale, and try to find thoughts that feel just a wee-bit better. As the Chinese philosopher Lao Tzu says, "the journey of a thousand miles begins with a single step." There are a number of excellent processes in "The Astonishing Power of Emotions" by Abraham-Hicks that will help you reach for that better feeling.

[5] As I mentioned earlier, the five closest people to you affect your income. I was as shocked the first time I heard that as you probably are if you hadn't heard it before. I swear, I didn't make this up. As Jim Rohn initially said, and I paraphrase, "your income is equivalent to the average of the five people closest to you." People such as Anthony Robbins repeat this constantly from stages all over the world. Test it out, make a list of the five people you're with the most and then come up with an average of all their incomes. Is this around where your income falls? Interesting, right?

This began to hit home for me as I began attending seminars. My initial draw to them was this incredible sense of well-being, one which is difficult to put into words. Calling it a feeling of well-being somehow seems inadequate. I'm just drawn to these growth courses and camps. At first, I didn't even know why. All I knew is that I felt so light at these things. And then I came to the realization that it's the energy which I'm drawn to, to these higher frequencies. Nowadays, I'm more conscious of the effect environment has on my life, and seek out like-minded individuals to surround myself with - people who enrich my life.

That's not to say you should cut ties with certain - if not most - of the people in your social circle immediately, though that probably wouldn't be a bad thing in many cases! In all seriousness, be mindful of who you allow to have an influence over you. Many advise that you should spend less time with those who are negative, and look to cultivate friendships with people who are progressive thinkers; people you can learn from and who add value to your life. I don't necessarily disagree with this, but find it somewhat abrupt. My take on this is a bit different though. I believe that when you start to work to change yourself and to seek continuous growth, the people and things around you must also change. It's as simple as that. I didn't consciously get rid of anyone from my life, though I've naturally drifted apart from some people, I've become friends with others, and some people disappeared altogether! So be mindful of your inner world and the outer world will take care of itself – or at least that has been my experience.

[6]I mentioned that by changing your thoughts you can change your life. And a big part of changing your thoughts is changing the way you speak, and vice versa. I say vice versa because internal dialogue, which

resembles the language you use to speak out loud, has an enormous effect on every aspect of your life. Words, whether spoken or thought, are really powerful because they create our reality. In the Bible it says that God created the universe first with a thought and then with the spoken word when he said, "Let There Be Light."

The more emotion behind the spoken word, the more powerful it is.

Use more positive language and steer away from negative talk (see section on complaining and gossip). I am so keenly aware of things that come out of my mouth, that sometimes I consider myself wound up a bit too tight. Amazing things are coming into my life though, and I can't help but notice the correlation. That goes for my thoughts as well, though I'm especially mindful of what I say out loud because of how it could affect other people. "We all face death in the end, but on the way, be careful never to hurt a human heart," said Rumi, the great Sufi poet. It's one of my favorite quotes and I take it to heart. Comments will slip by at times but I catch myself, and then I try to behave differently in the future. Oh - and this is very important - forgive yourself instead of beating yourself up for the things you say. So, what does your internal voice sound like?

In this section, I also want to mention the importance of keeping your word, both to others and to yourself. Even before I started getting involved in personal growth, broken promises (I call them promises but I'm referring to any and every commitment you make) were my biggest pet peeve. How can you trust someone who says one thing now but then does another, or doesn't follow through with what they say? Would you want to do business with someone like that? Me neither. Furthermore, if you can't keep your word to yourself, how can you ever believe in anything you say? Let me give you an example; if you say "I'm going to the gym later today," but you're too tired or too lazy to do so and end up staying home. You're right, nobody will know except you; but you'll be reinforcing the fact that you can't even trust yourself. This in turn affects your self-confidence and, by definition, all the decisions you make, which leads to less than desirable outcomes/conditions in your life.

Wealthy people practice what's called random disciplines. They commit to doing certain things just to strengthen the "discipline" muscle. A few months ago, I decided that I'd go to yoga at 7am three days a week, which isn't too early, except that I have a whole morning routine. It includes meditation, amongst visualizing and other things, so I have to be up substantially earlier than I'd like. Do I just roll over when the alarm goes off in the morning because I'm too tired? I could, and no one would care. But I care. For one, I really enjoy yoga and couldn't fit it into my schedule at a different time. But it's also a random discipline for me. I made a commitment to myself that

I'd be there whenever possible, and by following through, I am growing to trust myself on a deeper level than ever before.

[7] Space is necessary for all creation. Think of the things in your life – if you want new clothes, you must create space for them by getting rid of your old or fat clothes, or things you don't wear. Or you must let go of certain things to create the space, such as clearing clutter in your home. For example, how much junk mail do you have lying around?

Sometimes it might even mean letting go of what is good for what might be great. Hanging on to things because you may eventually need them comes from a "lack mentality." Trust that the universe will provide everything you need at the right time. This goes back to my second pillar of success.

To create space and leave room for attraction, I practice transcendental meditation. This is a form of meditation that involves the use of a mantra. There are many ways to meditate, though, so find what is most suitable for you. By meditating, you are creating space between your thoughts, and thereby lowering your resistant energy. In other words, you are practicing the art of allowing.

I was under the impression that the object of meditating is to stop thinking, or rather, to stop listening to the nagging voice in your head by focusing on something else, such as your breath, a specific word, a mantra, etc. While this is, in fact, what you're technically doing when meditating, what you *really* want to do is to become conscious of being conscious. Michael Singer explains this concept wonderfully in his the book The Untethered Soul. Observing what the mind is doing is much more effective at helping you achieve stillness than trying not to think. The point is, when you meditate - even for a few minutes - resistant thoughts stop and thereby allow the things you want to come into your life. I keep my meditation practice to about 20 minutes a day, although I know people whose daily regimen is two hours! I hear contradictory things with regards to the optimal amount of time to dedicate to meditating. I've heard opinions that range from all you need are fifteen minutes a day, to the longer the better. I have no idea what the right answer is - I think one should meditate for the amount of time that they can allot to their practice. Five minutes a day is better than none. If you're just starting out, maybe that's all you can comfortably do. You can gradually progress from there and feel it out.

Since beginning to meditate a few years ago, my demeanor has changed quite a bit. I'm more even tempered, and remain calm in the face of adversity. My general outlook on life is different, and solutions to problems are easier to see now that the "little me" is no longer at the forefront. I can now come from my higher self when giving situations color or meaning, and I don't let my mind take over and run away with me. I am in the driver's seat, and this consequently leads to better actions. I'm more mindful of how I behave toward situations and to others, and especially to how I treat myself - which goes back to the number one wealth principle in Julia Cameron's *The Artist's Way*: Treating yourself like a precious object will make you strong.

[8] A simple yet very powerful thing that will improve your life tremendously is to give up complaining. It sounds easy enough, but people oftentimes complain and they don't even realize they're doing it! My own mother did a great job of illustrating that exact point for me. One day, I put her on a complaint ban with the intention of experimenting and seeing how that would change her experience. So every time she began to complain within ear shot of me, I would clear my throat. And wouldn't you know? She was terribly surprised almost every time and said things like, "That was a complaint?!" Needless to say, I cut my social experiment short.

I'm not sure when I stopped complaining about things. To be honest, it's not something I habitually did even before discovering personal growth. Nowadays, I'm mindful to not so much as make a negative comment about the weather. It's pretty cool, when you don't complain little things become a non-issue.

So don't talk about how you don't like the rain or the cold, don't complain about your aches and pains to everyone you encounter, or comment on how so and so treated you unfairly. It will inevitably come into your mind, but why voice it? It neither helps you or the person taking it all in. Eventually, you won't even entertain negative thoughts for too long. If you're complaining all day, the universe will just give you more and more things to complain about. Remember, what you focus on expands. The reason complaining shapes your reality is because you are focusing your energy on something bad. This makes you put negative vibes out into the world and draws more negativity towards you.

One item I would add in this category that I think is often overlooked, or barely mentioned, is gossip. My advice is to steer clear of it because when you gossip you give out negativity and that's exactly what you get back. So gossip is not poisoning the person being gossiped about – it's actually only poisoning you! You don't make a correlation when you gossip about someone at lunch only to return to work to some major issue, for example. Or when you complain about your neighbor and then you get a flat tire. The good news is that the inverse is also true; when you sincerely speak highly of others or do nice things, there tends to be a positive correlation in your life – you help a friend move and the next day, your boss may give you tickets to a game, for example. Personally, the only time I really mention others is to speak well of them. If I have nothing good to say, I just don't say anything about them at all. If it's not positive, I noticed it tends to be gossip for the most part. Talking negatively about others is also a waste of energy.

The last thing I'd like to add in this section is that you should be sincerely happy for the successes and achievements of others as if they were your own. Admire the good qualities in others, and be happy for everything else that they may have that you desire for yourself. Being envious of them only pushes the things you want further away.

[9] It is somewhat challenging for me to write about this particular success pillar, because I feel like it's not my strong suit, but I do understand the importance of the power of focusing. The simplest way to explain it is to say that what you focus on expands, as I've mentioned throughout the book. Most people today are scattered and don't focus on what it is that they want – they suffer from a lack of focus, which is the number one obstacle to implementing the law of attraction. In the beginning, try focusing on the positive aspects of everything, and particularly in situations you perceive as being negative. Believe me, this gets easier with time. Try to become more specific in what you focus on as time goes on, such as aiming for certain things that you want to achieve.

Many teachers have used GPS as a great analogy, which goes something like this - your brain is like a GPS system in that if you tell it where you want to go, it will somehow get you there. But you have to be clear about where you're headed; otherwise the gadget has little use. The same goes for the things you want - how can you hit a target when you don't know what the target is? So get clear (focus on the target), and that way you'll have a much better chance of actually hitting it.

I can already hear you saying "*but I'm not sure what I wunt; I don't know what my purpose is,*" and that's ok. I went through, and continue to struggle with, the same thing. At an author's workshop, James MacNeil (author of Success Secrets of King Solomon, The Richest Man Ever), said, and I paraphrase, "never in a million years did I think I would be where I am now, doing what I do today. The trick is to know your next step and the road will pave itself before your eyes." Of course, this requires a degree of trust in the Universe, or whatever it is you believe in. It's a bit like driving at night, where you can only clearly see 100-200 feet ahead of you, but you know that the path leads somewhere.

In life though, there is no final destination. It's all about enjoying and getting as much juice as possible out of the ride.

[10] Last but not least, have you ever heard the saying that gratitude is the great magnifier? Whenever you are grateful for the things in your life, you are blessed with more things to be grateful about. Isn't it awesome how

that works? Gratitude is magnetic, and the more grateful you are, the more abundance you magnetize! Rhonda Byrne wrote a magnificent book all about the topic of gratitude called The Magic, and I highly recommend it. Just now I picked it up to read some passages again and decided I'm going to read it over. Why? Because I feel like I'm in a different place than the first time I read it and can have a deeper appreciation for it than I did when I first picked it up. That goes for most books by the way - I tend to read them more than once because I really want to get the most out of them; to truly internalize the author's teachings.

Expressing, and really feeling, gratitude can have a significant impact on your life. Your feelings magnetize more and more situations that cause more feelings of gratitude, and so on. It's like a vicious circle, except there's nothing vicious about it. The best times to think about the things you're thankful for are when you wake up and before falling asleep because, that's when your subconscious is the most receptive. There's an awesome free online gratitude journal at www.1thingapp.com, where you can list the things you're thankful for on any given day. On the site, you also have the option to upload one item per day into a common database, and then read things other users have expressed their thanks for - it's really neat. Another idea I like is having a gratitude rock; I have one (I got this idea from Rhonda Byrne), and each night I think of the thing from that day which I'm most grateful for right before falling asleep. There are so many ways you can apply gratitude in your life, for more ideas check out *The Magic* by Rhonda Byrne.

Gratitude also has the strongest link with mental well-being than any other character trait. It increases spiritualism, self-esteem, makes us more centered, improves sleep and increases energy levels. How's that for a good case?

When I look back at how far I've come, I'm filled with gratitude for life and everything in it. I never thought the day would come when I'd be saying this, but I'm actually glad for all that's happened; for going through my own personal hell and coming back from it. If none of that had happened, I would not be where I am today. I hope I can serve as an inspiration to someone going through some kind of personal trauma who cannot see the light at the end of the tunnel. Rest assured, there is a light, and one day you'll be able to look back and rejoice in the lessons you learned along the way. You are perfect in every moment, remember that.

Now go out and be the best you that you can be. The world is waiting.

Made in the USA
Lexington, KY
17 October 2015